Seeking the Elephant with Golden Tusks

By Sunshine Orange Studio

Translated by Zhao Mingzhen

Adapted by Joe Gregory

Books Beyond Boundaries

ROYAL COLLINS

Seeking the Elephant with Golden Tusks

By Sunshine Orange Studio
Translated by Zhao Mingzhen
Adapted by Joe Gregory

First published in 2022 by Royal Collins Publishing Group Inc.
Groupe Publication Royal Collins Inc.
BKM Royalcollins Publishers Private Limited

Headquarters: 550-555 boul. René-Lévesque O Montréal (Québec) H2Z1B1 Canada
India office: 805 Hemkunt House, 8th Floor, Rajendra Place, New Delhi 110 008

Original Edition © Yunnan Education Publishing House Co., Ltd.

ISBN: 978-1-4878-1020-7

To find out more about our publications, please visit www.royalcollins.com.

Once upon a time, there was a place called Mengbolan, ruled by King Supuman, a foolish and greedy man. An ordinary couple lived by a river in Mengbolan with a pair of lovely children. The son was Sunada, smart and brave, and his sister, Jianhong, who was eleven years younger. The family lived a happy life, full of laughter.

However, when Jianhong was learning to walk, their parents tragically passed away. Sunada took on the burden of looking after the household. The once so happy life turned hard.

One day, Jianhong was waiting as usual for her brother at home. It got later and later, and the sun was setting. Finally, Sunada appeared on the path. Jianhong ran down from their bamboo house toward her brother, waving at him!

Sunada was happy to see his sister. He gave her some delicious food wrapped in bamboo leaves and said, "Eat while it's hot." When she opened it and saw that it was grilled fish, she started crying. When her mother was still alive, she would often cook fish, and when Jianhong saw the fish, it made her miss her mom.

To make her happy, Sunada told her a story. "Once upon a time, there was a beautiful lake, with beautiful thousand-petal golden lotuses blooming. There was a forest by the lake, where a golden rooster would sing songs. When the golden rooster spread its dazzling golden wings and started singing lovely songs to the sun, the golden lotuses in the lake would bloom with brilliant golden light!"

Caught up in excitement from the story, little Jianhong stopped weeping.

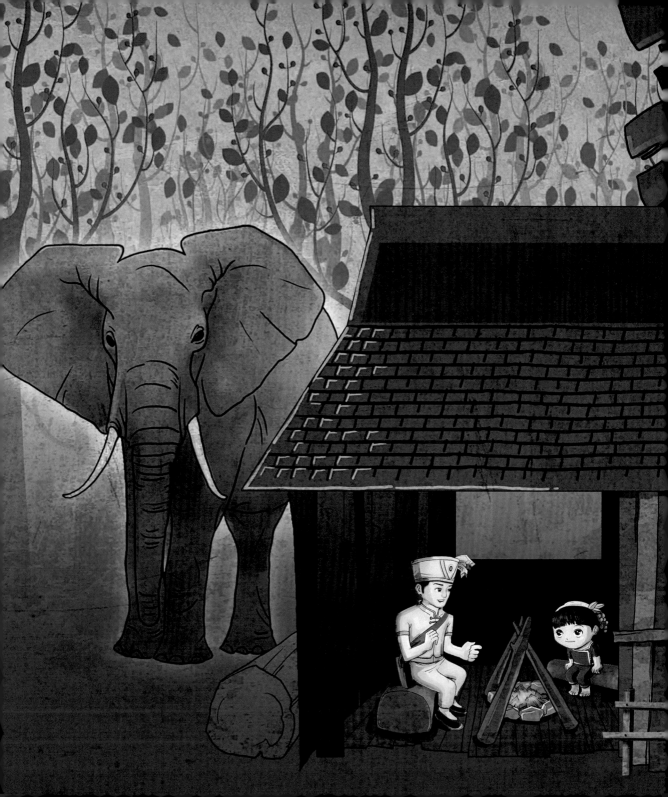

When Sunada told his sister about a special elephant with a pair of two glittering golden tusks, he was overheard by a well-known villain named Gadupi. Gadupi joyfully started making an evil plan.

The next day, Gadupi went to King Supuman and said, "Your Majesty, there are a brother and sister living by the riverside in the eastern part of your land. They can speak to animals, especially Sunada, the older brother. He can summon an elephant with golden tusks to carry them to the lakeside, so that they can listen to the golden rooster singing and watch a thousand-petal lotus glistening in golden light!" Upon hearing this, the king was stunned, and greedily licked his lips.

Realizing that he had tricked the king, he said again, "Your Majesty, you are the Lord of All Things. The elephant with golden tusks should belong to you, not that poor boy."

The king went to find the brother and sister. Although Sunada told him that he had just made up the story to make the sister happy, the king did not believe him. The king took Jianhong and demanded that the brother bring the elephant with golden tusks to him within seven days, or he would kill Jianhong.

Sunada felt angry and resentful. He burst into tears. Seeing this, the god Payaying was shocked. Filled with sympathy for the poor boy, Payaying decided to go down to the world to help him.

Feeling dizzy and with a heavy heart, Sunada walked into the deep forest, completely forgetting about all the ferocious beasts living there. He only worried about his sister in the palace. Suddenly, he heard the sound of flapping wings. Sunada saw a wounded little peacock. Feeling sorry for the bird, he helped the little peacock.

That evening, Sunada held the little peacock and put it into a hole in a tree to let it get some rest. After Sunada fell asleep, he had a dream where he saw the god Payaying with lucky clouds under his feet flying towards him. "My child, you have a heart of gold. You will get what you want!" With these words, Payaying left a jeweled sword and a pair of flying shoes. He told Sunada to fly to the east towards the rising sun.

The next morning, when Sunada woke up from his dream, he saw the jeweled sword and the flying shoes beside him. The peacock was gone. Carefully recalling his dream, he suddenly realized that the little peacock was the embodiment of Payaying. He confidently took the sword, and put the flying shoes on. He flew away towards the rising sun.

Sunada soon arrived at the Great Forest of Yimaban. He then found Palaxi, the most intelligent person in the forest. After hearing Sunada's story, Palaxi told him about King Dongpadong and his elephant with golden tusks. But because the king was imprisoned by demons, Palaxi had a plan to rescue the king.

The next day, Sunada bid farewell to Palaxi and left, with the jeweled sword on his back and flying shoes on his feet. He flew over dense forests and high mountains. Finally, he arrived in the Kingdom of Dongpadong.

Suddenly, just as Sunada went to lean against a big tree to take a rest, four fierce tigers jumped out from the bushes and attacked him. Sunada pulled out the jeweled sword and threw it at the tigers. The sword suddenly turned into a large fire cage, capturing the tigers. The tigers ran around in the fire cage, burning their skin and tearing up their flesh! Finally, the tigers were forced to go back to their original shapes, and Sunada realized that they were the four demons that had imprisoned King Dongpadong. Crying with pain, they begged for mercy.

Sunada drew the sword and cut down cane and rattan to tie up the four demons. The demons obediently took Sunada to the palace where King Dongpadong was imprisoned.

When the king saw Sunada's majestic and extraordinary appearance, he was very happy, and let his daughter, Princess Natani, marry Sunada.

On their wedding day, Princess Natani held up the token of lifelong love over her head—a golden lotus with a thousand petals—and threw it to Sunada. Sunada happily caught the beautiful flower and was lifted high by the people who had come to bless the newlyweds.

The following day, Sunada and Princess Natani carefully made up a detailed plan to rescue his sister.

Sunada and Natani went directly to Mengbolan, leading their troops over the mountains and through the forests. When the troops crossed the Great Forest of Yimaban, Sunada and Natani both said farewell to Palaxi and sincerely thanked him for the happiness he had given them. Then they continued to Mengbolan.